THE HALO

Also by C. Dale Young

Torn
The Second Person
The Day Underneath the Day

THE HALO

C. Dale Young

Four Way Books
Tribeca

Please direct all inquiries to:
Editorial Office
Four Way Books
POB 535, Village Station
New York, NY 10014
www.fourwaybooks.com

Library of Congress Cataloging-in-Publication Data

Young, C. Dale.
[Poems. Selections]
The halo / C. Dale Young.
pages ; cm
ISBN 978-1-935536-68-0 (pbk. : alk. paper)
I. Title.
PS3625.O96A6 2016
811'.6--dc23

2015028570

This book is manufactured in the United States of America and printed on acid-free paper.

Four Way Books is a not-for-profit literary press. We are grateful for the assistance
we receive from individual donors, public arts agencies, and private foundations.

This publication is made possible with public funds from the National Endowment for the Arts

and from the New York State Council on the Arts, a state agency.

[clmp]

We are a proud member of the Community of Literary Magazines and Presses.

Distributed by University Press of New England
One Court Street, Lebanon, NH 03766

To Jacob Bertrand,

& to the ever-changing vistas of memory

Contents

Eclipse   3

Enter the Dragon   5

Cuboidals   6

Annunciation   8

The Gods Among Us   10

Myth   12

The Hanged Man   14

An Ordinary Boy   15

The Prodigal   17

Mind Over Matter   18

The Ninth Metal   19

What Doesn't Kill You   21

The Master Plan   22

Bloodline   24

M. domestica   26

In flagrante delicto   28

After Crossing the *Via Appia*   30

The Second Fallacy   31

Hush   32

Wrestling with the Angel   33

Curio   35

Ruins   36

Instructions from Lazarus   37

What Is Revealed   38

In Pursuit   39

The Vista   41

By the Way   43

Learning to Walk   44

Praise 45
Epistle, Twenty-Five Years Too Late 47
The Sixth Sense 49
Money 51
The Wolf 53
Revelation 59
Human Wishes 61
The Halo 63

Ein jeder Engel ist schrecklich.

Every angel is terrifying.

—Rainer Maria Rilke

Eclipse

Admit it. You return to your past because you
have gained some kind of knowledge to interpret it:
the titanium device with its four pins meticulously
buried in your skull, sunlight from the window
reflecting off its edges to cast fractured lines of light

across your chest and across your hospital bed,
these rays of light appearing to beam from this metal ring
around your head (like a goddamned angel), or
how when your nurse flicks it with his plastic pen
it vibrates in a key you cannot yet name. Call it

the key of metal, of titanium, of shiny misfortune.
Admit it, the present is awfully dull and will remain so
until many years later when it comes miraculously
into focus, when you understand all four meanings
of the word *regret*. So it is you go back, armed now

with this word *halo*, word rife with what
you have learned about how angels were depicted
in Renaissance painting, the ring or rings of light painted
by the old masters so as to hover lightly around the head.
And how can you not see with this knowledge, knowing

as you do now about those terrible wings you keep
and continue to keep secret? Some would argue
we keep secrets because we cannot help ourselves.
But what if secrets are kept simply because we have yet
to make sense of what really happened?

The moon in latest afternoon, just days ago, hid
a segment of the setting sun, and there before us a *mandorla*
without even a faint sketch of a god or angel beneath it.
Admit it, I am not alone: things beg for significance.
Would that we always had time to come back to them. . .

Enter the Dragon

To move is to experience pain. To turn
my head, impossible. My neck bone shattered
as easily as a glass window, and that cord,
my spinal cord, knew its fortress of bone
had been weakened by assault. My room,

in its mottled greys, smelled like Lysol,
smelled like a bitter chemical of cleanliness.
To say "trapped" would be imprecise.
To say "restrained" would be a misnomer.
On the television hung in the corner

of my hospital room, Bruce Lee entered the dirt
courtyard, his arms cycling and cycling,
his cry a warning to the men circling the pit.
"Enter the Dragon." I had seen it before.
But I was not Bruce Lee. I was a man

broken by Bruce Lee's leaping hands—hands
to the head, hands to the neck. And I know
now that a cracked bone is not necessarily
a broken bone. I know that now. I have studied
long enough to become one of those men who stood

by my bed in white coats. Still, when I go back,
there is the Dragon and broken glass, the vertebra
shattered, my body forced to lie still. I know better now.
I know how to throw my voice, how to lie, to reassure
someone he will live, that he will, in fact, not die.

Cuboidals

I dream a dream of silence and prickly weeds,
same weeds they found on my shirt
as I lay in the grass, same dream that stank
of chlorophyll and excrement. Infirm bed,
tightly-fitted bed, in that bed I was laid to rest,

what better than sleep? What better than dream?
Dream a loosened sheet, a crumpled sheet.
I could move that sheet in my mind
but my body stayed still. Dream of autumn
in Florida. Dream of car spin and glass,

my body wracked by fever and wings
suddenly breaking through the skin between
my shoulder blades. Cuboidals, yes,
small squares of muscle found there
patiently waiting. Yes, the skin stretches.

Yes, it tears, the wings inside no longer
able to remain hidden. I was a monster,
sick monster, whose wings were spewing
from his back. The blades of these shoulders
could not clip them. They rose from my back

so quickly I was pushed up from my bed.
But that sheet, it was a careful netting
placed to hold this dirty bird down, to keep it
in check. Terrible, these wings, and longer
than my entire length. The dream

always starts with the sound of breaking glass,
the still surprising smell of burning rubber. Dream
of paper birds on the wall, birds tacked into place.
Even now, my wings are twitching. Who will
hold me down now, restrain me like an animal?

Annunciation

I learned to hide my wings almost immediately,
learned to tuck and bandage them down.
Long before the accident, before the glass shattering
and that scene going dim, dimmer, and then dark,
before the three fractures at the axis, three cracks

in the bone, it had already begun. My voice
had begun to deepen, the sound of it
suddenly more my father's than my own. My beard
had started growing, my bones growing, my bones
sore from the speed of their growth, and there,

at fourteen years of age, the first tugging
of the muscles between my shoulder blades.
It began as a tiny ache. It was just a minor irritation.
Day after day passed, and this ache grew,
and then the tips of the cartilaginous wings

began to tent my skin. Father Callahan
had already warned that in each of us
there was both potential for bad and good.
When trying to shave for the first time, I nicked
my cheek, the bleeding slow but continuous.

Standing there, dabbing at this small cut with tissue paper,
the first tear surprised me, the left wing heaving through
that fleshy mound of muscle between my shoulder blades
and then the skin. I buckled and, on my knees, the right wing
presented itself more rapidly than the left.

When I stood, there in the mirror, my wings outstretched
with their tiny feathers wet, almost glutinous, a quick
ribbon of blood snaking down my back. You wonder
why I am such a master of avoidance, such a master
of what is withheld. Is there any wonder, now?

I had no idea then they would wither and fall off
in a few weeks. When Father Callahan patted
my head in the sacristy and told me I was
a good boy, a really good boy, an extraordinary boy,
I wanted to be anything but extraordinary.

The Gods Among Us

One of them grants you the ability
to forecast the future; another wrenches
your tongue from your mouth, changes you
into a bird precisely because you have been
given this gift. The gods are generous

in this way. I learned to avoid danger, avoid fear,
avoid excitement, these the very triggers that prompt
my wings from their resting place deep inside.
And so, I avoided fights, avoided everything really.
In the locker room, I avoided other boys,

all the while intently studying that space
between their shoulder blades, patiently looking
for the tell-tale signs, looking to find even
one other boy like me, the wings buried but
there nonetheless. I studied them from a distance.

When people challenge a god, the gods curse them
with the label of madness. It is all very convenient.
And meanwhile, a god took the form of a swan
and raped a girl by the school gates. Another
took the shape of an eagle to abduct a boy

from the football field. Mad world.
And what about our teachers? Our teachers
expected us to sit and listen. In Theology, there was
a demon inside each of us; in History,
the demons among us. So many demons

in this world. Who among us could have spoken up against the gods, the gods who continued living among us? They granted wishes and punishments much the way they always had. Very few noticed them casually taking the shape of one thing or another.

Myth

Someone had placed his hands on me,
my limp body a stubborn testament to an accident.
But then the toes moved. My toes curled. A dream?
No dream. My toes flexed, and then my left knee
bending, bending, then bent. I have no other explanation.

Yes, yes, the brain is capable of incredible lies.
I have seen how a damaged eye, a damaged
portion of retina, incapable of interpreting light, can be
suppressed by the brain, the brain literally painting
over a blank spot in someone's vision.

The brain is capable of beautiful lies; it hums
its songs softly. My toes curled, my leg shifted, and
in a fit of what—anger? love?—I lifted my arms, bent
my back, rose up from the bed at the waist.
Did anyone see this? Did they see this monster

rise from the bed? My legs shifted, my legs flopped
over the side of the bed. And when I stood, my knees
no longer understood the weight of me. My knees
buckled predictably, this body quietly falling to the floor.
All heard was the whistle of the halo scraping tile.

In a dream I had once, I watched my hands
burn, fire's tongues flickering up from my palms.
Lying on the floor, my skin burned in that room.
No fire, but my nerves misfiring. I laughed. I laughed
harder than I ever had before, chest-hurting laughter.

The monster lived. The monster crumpled on the floor
but alive nonetheless. And when my nurse arrived,
commotion came with him. There were his hands again,
lifting me back into bed. The old me was dead and gone.
Fire, hands, and songs hummed softly—this monster had risen.

The Hanged Man

I know a lot about the second cervical vertebra.
And because I love precision and accuracy, I refer
to it as the axis, its name buried in Latin,
meaning *chariot*, meaning *axle*, meaning the line
around which something revolves or turns.

How is that for being exact? And to break the axis,
to fracture it, is rare. A neurosurgeon will tell you
it comprises only 15% of cervical spine injuries.
Although we live in the 21st century and one
would assume a more clinical name for breaking

the axis, such a break is still called the Hangman's
Fracture. I need not explain the derivation
of such a name. Not divers or thrill-seekers,
but heretics and those charged with treason
provided such a term—the hanged man, the monster,

the witch and the unloved. Go ahead; break this bone.
Shatter it. Leave cracks to be seen on an x-ray.
The hanged man walking tilts his head to the side
opposite the cracks. He tilts his head away from
such an insult. He tries to appear normal.

But there is no name for such behavior,
no clinical name to describe this odd activity of avoidance.
I have spent years studying avoidance. I am
an expert now. I never say the hip bone is connected
to the thigh bone. I say acetabulum, say head of the femur.

An Ordinary Boy

A fascicle of feathers in my hand, hand
frantic and shaking, my arm holding my hand
as far away from my body as possible—I am disgusted.
I cannot pull out the central stalks of my wings
where they protrude from between my shoulder blades,

but I can strip every tuft of feathers from them
to bare those cartilaginous stems as they rise
from my back, stalks stripped perfectly
clean so as to better tuck them along my spine,
hide them, make them invisible beneath my clothing.

I was so foolish then, a teenager not yet able
to accept what he was. When my wings blackened,
withered, and fell off, I was beyond happy.
They would stay dormant sometimes as long as
three months. Sadly, they always came back.

In the bathroom mirror, I can see myself offering
a cluster of feathers to myself, as if to say:
Take this from me and I will be forever grateful.
But the me that is a trick of light on glass
is uncaring, offers them back immediately.

If I concentrate, if I think hard on it, I can move
my wings, and I practice in the bathroom mirror.
But these wings cannot support my weight,
cannot buoy me on even a strong gust of wind.
What good are wings if you cannot fly?

What good is this ridiculous secret I am asked
to keep? With the feathers ripped cleanly away,
I tuck the stems along my spine. I bandage them down—
cloth wound under my armpits, tightly wound
around my chest. I fashion myself into an ordinary boy.

The Prodigal

Yes, the winds must have picked up, must have
slowed the motion of my car or the other one that missed
the red light. Not strong enough, these winds, to have
kept either car out of the intersection, but enough. . .
When I go back, when I return to the scene, I am

18 and worried. I was always worried, this thing
inside me growing , this "unnatural" urge to take
a man's face in my hands and kiss his mouth
almost violently. And maybe the gods knew this.
Maybe the gods wanted to show me death is death

whether by accident, by fire, or by festering disease.
But for those three minutes, the world broke
from its axis, and that intoxicated woman missed
the light. There was the sound of breaking glass
and the smell of burning rubber, and then deep sleep.

I go back. I go back to watch myself materialize in the bed,
to watch the panic on my face, the halo with its nails in my head
something monstrous and beautiful like the very works
of the gods. I was not dead. I would eventually move—this body,
this world, returned to its almost original axis.

Mind Over Matter

Things repeat themselves—mirror themselves—
sometimes with only a slight variation, the edges
of a bloom, perhaps, tinged in rust instead of alizarin.
But the bloom remains the same. Just so, the lily
repeats itself each spring, surprising even the shrubbery

in Golden Gate Park with its shock of white, at times
milk white. I have photographs to prove this, photographs
in which these blooms each year appear in almost the same place.
It is like magic, dark magic. No one can explain it to me.
Which theorem helps us understand how these blooms

arrive again and again in similar and predictable spaces?
Once upon a time, I watched motion-capture photography
bring a flower's previous bloom back to sit in view
of its current incarnation. Ah, the miracle of optics
and the science of a dark room. Once upon a time,

I woke to find myself cradled in a bed, the hospital room
streaked with light and shadow from half-opened blinds.
I tried to move but could not. I saw the metallic light
reflected from the halo around my head. I saw a doctor
standing by my bedside studying me, his furrowed brow

tempered by a half-smile. As my eyes grew accustomed
to the light, this doctor faded away. The brain can lie,
but this was no trick. The man standing over me was me.
This man had come to assure me I would live, that I
would become the very man I did not want to become.

The Ninth Metal

Who could fault a child for wanting to fly?
Exhibit 1: comic books. They are crammed with
heroes that fly: Green Lantern, Iron Man and,
of course, the ubiquitous Superman. I'm not crazy.
And I am not that naïve. Men aren't supposed to fly.

Men aren't supposed to have wings. And even as a child,
before my own wings had first erupted, I knew this.
But what does one do with Hawkman? Hawkman
with his wings? Hawkman flying with his wings extended?
I have learned a lot about flight since then, learned that

Hawkman's flying was never a result of his wings.
Which child understands the physics of the *ninth metal*?
You know, that metal Hawkman has in his boots,
his belt, etc.? It defies gravity at the mind's will.
I hate Hawkman. I mean, how advantageous

for this man with wings to also have this means
of defying gravity. I'm not crazy, but for years
I believed Hawkman actually used his wings to fly.
What is seen clearly is not always understood clearly.
See, Hawkman's lie is the most egregious

of these heroes that fly. None of the others have wings.
None of them. Seriously. Men aren't meant to fly.
And on the roof of my house in late afternoon
so many years ago, my wings newly erupted and
extended to full wingspan, I did not triumph over gravity.

Since then, I have learned to control my wings, learned
to hide them. I don't want to fly. I am more than a bird.
I am more than these wings I never asked for.
I am just a man no longer trying to defy
gravity's insistent pull, to defy his own sad story.

What Doesn't Kill You

makes you stronger, they say. But stronger than what?
Thrice, three times, a trio of cracks— the vertebra
with its three indiscretions, three breaks in the cement
of my neck, one for each of my turns across the asphalt.
See, you have to be bad to the bone to survive

such an accident, to wake up this way. The good
get damaged, and the good stay damaged. The good
carry sunshine and hope. They die. They don't get
stronger. They die. *Rise from fire, rise from
broken glass and detritus, you monster.* There are three

fates: one who weaves the thread, one who measures it,
and one who cuts it. Three times the Doctor held
his penlight to my eyes to watch my pupils constrict.
Good, I thought I was good; I thought I was dead.
But I was alive. Alive and stronger. Stronger?

Some kind of strength, right? My left hand incapable
of movement. My other hand moving without
direction. The good are damaged and stay damaged.
I am hurt and want to rise from this bed, its sheets
like fire on my legs. Three times I try to move.

Three times I curse the gods. Three times I curse myself
for cursing the gods. A filthy light reflects off the edge
of my halo. How very saintly of me to wear a halo.
The light flickering and burning around my head—
I check my own pupils; I dare myself to get the fuck up.

The Master Plan

But memory is the greatest lie of all. No,
correction: greatest set of lies. Even the boy
who remembers his mother reading to him is
participating in lies. So it is that to recollect
a god pinning me to my hospital bed,

his hands cruel against my chest, his beard
dangling only mere inches away from my lips,
my inability to move, the weight of him
crushing me against the bed as he whispers
Who are you to question the divine? is nothing more

than memory, a lie. The nerves in my neck and back
on fire, prickly heat rippling through me like fire?
A lie. It was nothing more than nerves misfiring.
The metal ring, the titanium ring around my head,
the halo—was sadly, most definitely, not a lie.

One misfortune begets another. And all stories
of origin are lies that beget more lies. Three cracks
in the axis begets the halo. The halo begets a state
of stillness, or is that begat? Stillness
allows my wings to erupt uncontrollably

from my back. I prefer to think that this was the sequence
of events, injury. . . halo. . . stillness. . . that birthed the monster.
But that, too, is a lie. My wings had made themselves
known years earlier, had erupted to full span and withered
away many times before. Who am I to question the divine?

Who am I to return to this scene armed with words
and bookish learning? I sit here now with my wings
about to rupture the tissues between my shoulder blades.
I want answers, meaning I want lies. I want lies.
I muck around in memory and find only lies.

Bloodline

In that old story, the boy is depicted as delicate,
lithe, and beautiful. Ovid had it wrong.
Yes, the boy was beautiful, beautiful enough
to capture a god's attention, but he was not
delicate. He was anything but delicate,

his muscles toned from working the fields.
Listen to me; the gods are fairly conventional.
A lovely woman is transformed into
an old hag, a too-slow voyeur becomes
the quick stag to be chased and shot through

by a single arrow. So, in the case of this young man,
he must have been strong, anything but delicate
like these flowers. The gods are convincing
when they need to be. Believe me, they are
honey-mouthed and persistent. The boy

had to be strong, but he was not stronger than the gods.
He was seduced; who isn't seduced by
immortality? In the field, the boy was every bit
the archer as the god. He was just as powerful
with a spear, a slingshot, or a discus.

Ovid writes that Apollo loved the boy,
loved him more than any living thing
on this earth. But we know better.
The gods love only themselves. In the field,
a clearing ringed by trees, the boy did not

try to catch the discus. He was running from it,
running from the god who took pains to aim
so as to slice him clean through with a single shot.
You see, this is not love. A god commanding
spilled blood become delicate blue flowers is not love.

M. domestica

How could this have happened?
Bound to a bed, incapable of turning my head,
this man, still a boy, who had never been still?
Simple enough, the answer: a car running
a red light, a car colliding with my own car,

and then days gone missing. And then
days in which a week passed within 24 hours.
And then the fly that crawled on my nose,
less a fly than an itch I couldn't scratch, an itch
I refused to scratch out of some challenge

to myself to be stronger than that, to see
if my mind could suppress such a basic instinct.
I wanted to be better than that, wanted to
overcome the humiliation of that bed,
the humiliation of sickness, my own

foolish body's failings. The fly on the window,
the fly circling before my eyes preparing, again,
to perch on my nose or face. It would be a few years
before I formally met the fly, *Musca domestica*,
its wings papery and almost-seen-through

under a dissecting microscope, just a few years
before I would manipulate swabs and glass
to hold the fly down while extracting lysozymes
with the smallest of pipettes, my hands
suddenly calm and purposeful. As each

fly died in my initial attempts, I felt the itch subside
a little more. I hated the fly, hated its love
of filth, how it licked all of those dirty surfaces,
its horrid proboscis, its oddly-jointed legs.
I tell you, that itch is almost imperceptible now.

In flagrante delicto

An itch, and then that prickly
heat, the pointed tips
at the wings' terminus tenting
the skin between my shoulder blades.
I was so young then—pain,

that ripping sensation and that sound
as those points compromised the
muscle, as they tore through my skin.
The wings erupted. My wings
spewed from my back. I expected

blood to splatter, but in the mirror
the tiled floor behind me
remained clean. And as my
wings extended, I saw
that the greyish feathers

were clean. No one can recreate
the panic of the first time.
Some would say I am crazy,
that this was just a dream.
But it was no dream. Over a lifetime,

I have become a Master
of concealment. I have learned to tuck
my wings, learned to wear two shirts
until the wings blacken, wither, and
fall off. I don't even know why

I am telling you this. I shouldn't be
telling you this. But there are times
like this one where, standing naked,
I try to deploy them, anxious
to show the very things that

used to terrify me. I open
my shoulders. I lean forward. I wait.
Go ahead. Put your arms around me.
Press your warm fingers
into my back. There. Right there.

After Crossing the *Via Appia*

One must never trust in hearing. One should trust,
instead, in the smell of burning rubber,
the sight of glass shattering and then rushing away
from your very skin, skin vibrating the way it does
before sex or after a light rain. Because. . . . Because.

Because my wings had already erupted from between
my shoulder blades. Because I had coveted
another man in that secret space in my own head,
the lean shape of him, his water-drenched skin as he rose
from the sea off Fort Lauderdale Beach. Because I

had been weak, had questioned Father Callahan
about the body of Christ. One should not covet.
Thou shalt not covet. And who was I to question
the workings of the divine? Thou shalt not question
things that are holy and beyond question.

Because Aquinas, too, had been on the Appian Way.
Because he, too, had hit his head and would never
be loved by the divine. Because he could not
be trusted, because he knew too well the teachings
of Aristotle. Because he lied in that way we all lie.

In that bed in which I lay motionless, my mind could not
comprehend the fire felt but not visible. Even now,
one wants to interrogate, to call on the wide sky above
and ask it *why*. The simple mind never learns its lesson.
It never learns. It never learns. It never learns.

The Second Fallacy

You despise it, the bougainvillea, so you plant it
on either side of your front door. You call this luxury.
It is a very specific type of luxury. The bougainvillea
asks for nothing. It methodically climbs beside
your front door. You have charted this. You

cannot help yourself. You have watched this plant
so many times that it comforts you. My mother
planted them at the edge of her yard so many years ago
because one's eye trains itself without training
on the hot-pink petals—leaves, really—seen

more clearly against a dark and rotting fence.
And you find that no matter how far you push backward,
no matter how hard you pressure memory, you cannot
remember any image earlier than this one in your life.
Not her warm hands or the early pleasure of milk.

Not the first time she read to you. What you return to
are the terrible wings rising from your own back, your heart
a panicked bird beating within the slick pericardium.
As far back as you go, nothing before those petals.
You think you have learned something about tenderness,

but what have you really learned? Memory
refuses to yield. Memory will not be tortured
into submission. Not tenderness in the eye but
the brute need to see accurately. You know
this is a terrible thing to admit. You know this now.

Hush

Anyone can kiss me. Anyone
can pin my face with two hands and
kiss me hard. As with much in life, it
has taken me a long time to understand this.
I study so many things: how a hawk's wings

when stretched allow them to dry faster;
how an extract of the foxglove reduces
the results of a failing heart, can alter vision
if taken in excess, something Van Gogh understood
without understanding the exact mechanism.

You would expect me, at this point, to reference
something from Greek Antiquity, but I won't.
No need. Anyone can kiss me, but this does not mean
anyone wants to, does not mean anyone wants to
change my bandages when my terrible wings

are decaying, their feathers blackening and falling off,
the dark blood inscribed on the bandages and sheets.
Who on earth wants a man more monster than angel?
I lie face down while you remove my bandages
and clean up the mess. Nothing a little rubbing alcohol

can't clean up, you say. And when you finish, when you
bend and kiss the rotting wings between my shoulder blades,
I have nothing to say. But I need something to say.
Even now, I still need something better to say
than this hush love creates between two people.

Wrestling with the Angel

after Leon Bonnat

First off, those wings were too perfect.
Secondly, that the angel is both pushing the man
with his left hand while embracing him with his right,
his right leg stretching away from the man while
his left is anchored and wrapped between

the man's legs, his pelvis locked to the man's
left hip, only the man's loincloth of fur separating them,
the angel hoisted by the man's powerful embrace—
nothing remotely erotic about this; nothing at all. . . .
Both are muscular, though this man, who must be

named Jacob, is slightly more so. This embrace,
we are told, is neither classical in its presentation
nor remotely realistic, this man and this angel
joined belly to chest, the sweat on their skins a glue.
I would be lying if I said I only noticed this casually,

how Jacob's lifting of the angel is counterbalanced by
the angel's resistance, how it almost looks like a dance.
I would be lying if I said I wasn't excited by the sight
of those two almost naked male bodies struggling:
in the museum of adolescence, this is hardly unexpected.

But it was the wings of the angel that irritated me.
Those wings, mandarin fans, plucked from
an oversized swan, were just too perfect. No one can
convince me that Bonnat did not study swans to paint
those wings. He must have. They are swans' wings,

not the kind of wings that spring from between
shoulder blades, not the ones with tufts of grey feathers,
more quill-like than fan-like, wings. . . well, like mine.
The curator droned on about the myth. So few of us
knew this backlit story lost in the desert ages ago.

Curio

What monster is so easily caught, so easily
burned? There was a fire in my bed, a fire
in my chest, and the boy who inhabited this fire,
this monster, could not move, was held down,
held down and held accountable.

Fire consumed my hospital room, digested
its sterile air. . . (Why should an accident
live on in the mind?) I tell you now to trap
the car. Trap the boy. Burn everything. Pin
the remains, pin them like moths to the felt wall

of a curio. Subdue him. Make of him a memento.
Force him to contend with stillness—light,
fire, the halo and its clean metal gleam. Kill this sick
monster, poor captured monster. You must never forget
this monster can kill a man. It can even kill itself.

Ruins

The sand dotted with trash and detritus,
and out over the horizon that first hint of light
betrayed sunrise was coming, the Atlantic
not as wine dark as it had been an hour earlier.
One walks among ruins to remind oneself

that progress is made at any cost. You
had come to the beach late the night before
because a man had promised you
he could walk on water, had promised
to show you this, you doubting Thomas.

You believed his gin-soaked detailing,
believed he could slowly and carefully float out
over water, and you thought he was like you.
But all he did was walk on the sand, earth-bound
and unbalanced. He had neither wings

nor the ability to fly. And when he removed
your shirt and felt the stumps between your
shoulder blades, your wings dormant, buried beneath
your flesh, he wanted to show you every ability he had
except that of flight. People lie. Lessons like these

are always difficult. A reckless sun tilted at the edge
of the horizon, and then the gulls arrived to begin
their studies, their lonely scavenging.
And my small lesson? Human to want the company
of others, and human, too, to find loneliness among them.

Instructions from Lazarus

Having risen from bed, after my ability
to stand had been re-established, my gait still
adjusting to the shifts of my body's weight,
I found myself in front of the streaked mirror
in my hospital room. The halo was dull

in that light, almost brushed in appearance.
How saintly of me to wear a halo.
I wanted a narrator to say: *Here, he models*
our latest headwear, the finest in German engineering.
But James Earl Jones was apparently unavailable.

The pins buried in my skull made me look like
a nautical device of some kind. Unfortunately,
there were no journeys for me, just a bed and a room.
My nurse's name was Zar, short for Lazarus.
Of course his name was Lazarus. It fits with the

theme of this whole thing. Zar said take it easy,
said move slowly and think about each step
as if you are learning to walk. But one doesn't
think about each step when learning to walk.
We rise, we fumble, we shuffle, and we fall.

My wings, buried (thankfully), were just an itch
between my shoulder blades, a slight tug
on those muscles depending on the way I moved.
Each night I prayed to make it out of the hospital
before they made themselves known again.

What Is Revealed

Even a Master who possesses an indisputable style
can be troubled by doubt and pride
in the same moment. Buonarotti, so enraged
that some who had seen his *Pietá* believed
it had been sculpted by someone else,

returned to his sculpture and claimed it as his own:
MICHAEL ANGELUS BONAROTUS FLORETIN FACIEBAT
chiseled across the sash on the Virgin's chest.
None of his other sculptures make such a pronouncement.
Standing in front of his statue, shielded now

by bullet-proof glass, one envisions the madman
with a pick-axe attacking it screaming "I am
the Christ, and I am alive!" So many of us
have these odd ideas in our heads.
We say men like this have schizophrenia

because we aren't sure what else to say.
Much of this world remains hidden, and
all the science in the world cannot illuminate
every dark corner, much less the corners of the mind.
I tuck my wings along my spine. I wear two shirts. I

keep my wings hidden. We accept that things must be so,
that somewhere in the back of the statue a piece of marble
is missing (the Virgin's nose had to be reconstructed).
We accept. And we doubt. And we hide things.
After thousands of years, very little has changed.

In Pursuit

Her feet, at first racing through the trees
with the quickness of an antelope, her body
throwing itself forward, hurling itself, the speed
of it like a drug, the speed of it
a necessary thing to escape the god

—no one has yet to convince me her father's response
to her cries for help was a blessing—then her feet
slowing and denser, growing heavy, heavy,
then fixed, her toes curling into the dirt
and taking root, the bark rising up

from the surface of her skin, her skin
prickling and tender as the bark restrained her,
her arms suddenly captured in the motion of surrender,
her arms held out on either side of her,
her hair falling out and then leaves,

newly green, almost silver, ripping through
her skin, through the bark, the leaves delicate and fine,
leaves marking her not as a young woman but as
a tree, a laurel tree, the very leaves torn from her and
fashioned into a crown by the god.

So few of these transformations are ever a blessing.
So, it isn't as if I had been lacking preparation.
You could say I had studied for it, sat patiently
with those old metamorphoses for years. My
shy hunter has never read these tales, would

likely find them silly. What he says is *See that grouse
over there? Shoot it.* And I do. I don't even
question it. Sometimes, my skin feels prickly,
and I wonder if another transformation is about
to take place. But no one is ever transformed twice.

No one. Ovid understood this. Even Suetonius
understood this. The gods have little use for us once
we have been changed. They take the laurel leaves,
scorn the wounded bird, erase their tell-tale footprints,
busy themselves with the generous work of gods.

The Vista

Not tenderness in the eye but a brute need
to see accurately: over the ridge on a trail
deep in Tennessee, the great poet looked out
and examined the vista that confederate soldiers saw
as they rode over its edge rather than surrender.

I saw only the cliff's edge and then
estimated the distance down to the bottom
of that dirty ravine. This is what someone with wings
does when he knows he cannot fly: he measures
distance. I have spent far too much time

examining my wings in the bathroom mirror
after the shower's steam has evaporated
from the medicine cabinet's toothpaste-spattered glass:
grey, each feather just slightly bigger than a hawk's.
The great poet said one might find a vista like this,

perhaps, once in a lifetime, but I didn't understand
what he meant by this then. My wings, tucked
beneath my t-shirt, beneath my long-sleeved oxford,
my wings folded in along my spine, were irritated
by that humid air, itchy from collecting sweat after hiking.

I wasn't paying attention, which is a sin I have since learned.
At 14, after the wings first erupted from my back,
I went up to the roof and tried to fly. Some lessons
can only be learned after earnest but beautiful failures.
My individual feathers are just slightly bigger than a hawk's

feathers. My wingspan is just about 8 feet. I'm a man,
and like men I measure everything. But vistas
make me nervous. And the great poet made me nervous.
And I knew then what I still know now, that I
was only seconds away from another beautiful failure.

By the Way

You are right to point out the agapanthus
is not a lily, especially to one who so loves
precision, but the agapanthus is also called
"Lily of the Nile," which surely could be seen
as justification for calling it a lily.

I am sure Cleopatra herself never called
this plant agapanthus. And, well, wouldn't one
want to be more like Cleopatra than like
Theophrastus? The Queen of the Nile
would have likely called it a lily, no?

Yes, yes, words have meaning and have power
and all of that stuff. Yes, yes, I of all people
understand the importance of naming.
But if Cleopatra would have called it a lily. . .
Okay, I'll stop. You look great, by the way.

But I just want to point out that the agapanthus
is such an odd plant that even botanists
cannot agree on the number of species in the genus,
some saying six, others as many as ten.
Okay, I swear I'll stop. Seriously. Promise.

The windy night air is cold, and my wings
are bound along my spine, sweaty and bruised,
these long bandages chafing my armpits. Words
have power, my love. You call this winged thing
an angel, but that is not the word I would use for it.

Learning to Walk

The halo, still fixed to my head then,
pinned to my calvarium's fine table
of bone, almost helped me to balance.
And balance is such a fine quality.
No matter how many times my mother

recounts for me how I first learned
to walk, I have no recollection of it.
But I remember my second time,
because learning to walk as an adult,
like learning anything one should learn

as a child, involves shame and embarrassment,
those despicable sisters who love to watch you fail.
To clutch two poles alongside you, poles
parallel to the ground you stand on, you wish
you were a gymnast or at least studying

to be a gymnast. Instead, you feel
the terrible weight of yourself grappling with
the weight of yourself, one final and awful
proof for gravity. Shouldn't a man who has wings
be immune from such things, be immune from gravity?

Shouldn't he be able to hover in place,
his wings vibrating like a bee's wings do?
That need to stand, that desperate need to walk,
was embarrassing. I said so many prayers then.
I prayed to any god I thought would listen.

Praise

The hawk need not measure distance.
It need not estimate its time from drift or glide
to the lightning bolt necessary to pluck
a chick from the edge of the yard.
Apollo's messenger, his cleanest predator—its beak

is perfect, its talons perfect, its hunger and its
manipulation of air perfect. You have to respect
the hawk. Over the field, I watch one circle and circle
tracing the symbol for infinity. Even at this
distance, I can see the rustling grass

that betrays not wind but an animal.
From the movement of the long grass, I
predict rodent, field rat. And when the infinite,
those connecting circles of sway and glide
become lightning, become strike, it happens

in mere seconds. One spies the rodent's shape
clutched in the talons of that incredible machine.
We all have talents, gifts some call them.
Some of us live out our entire lives
blissfully unaware of these so-called gifts.

I can measure distance. I can estimate
distance from one thing to another,
from hawk to the *terra firma* of the field,
from one person to another. This is what
someone with wings does when he knows

he cannot fly. I respect the hawk. It
is a machine, Apollo's cleanest predator, his
gentle reminder. When my shy hunter stands
at the edge of the field, I scan the distance between us.
I wish to be silent in this air. I wish to be lightning.

Epistle, Twenty-Five Years Too Late

Let me explain. I never meant to cause you
trouble, you a master of wit and urbanity,
you who called me angel in the dark
corner of your terrace, your smile
anything but angelic. Keep control,

I thought, those two words in my head
a prayer, like two marbles turning
over and over in one's palm. Keep control.
The cocktail party sedate by then, its conversations
and laughter filtering through the screened door,

I was more than aware you were seducing me. I
let you seduce me, fine distraction that you were.
Outside, the air had only the slightest chill
on it, and try as I might, I could not effect
my usual chilliness. I rolled a prayer

around in my head. And when you put
your hand under my shirt joking that my chest
was like that of the marble torso of Apollo, only
a god or goddess could have saved me. Keep control.
Keep control of me. Could you do that? Control

this monster? Your lips, stained by wine, tasted
like wine, left wine stains on my neck. I
wanted. I wanted to stay with you instead of
retreating to Boston, to my cinder-block room.
When my wings started to twitch and ache,

I knew control was the last thing of which
I was capable. I should have stayed. I should have
let you have your way, let my terrible wings unfurl,
my wings like something in one of your poems, those
intricate machines of delicacy and controlled measures.

The Sixth Sense

I am reminded a dove is often heard before
it is seen, reminded that a rifle is an extension of
the man. I am reminded of so much this morning,
the rifle's weight awkward in my hands.
Lock the target, sense the line, let the gun

do its job. Must everything in life
sound so mystical? Out in the field
two wild turkeys mope and saunter;
they know we are after birds of the air and not
those that prefer the field. I am reminded that

we are also creatures that prefer fields.
Trust your hearing, I am told. But my hearing
isn't my best sense. And that keen sense of sight
I inherited seems strangely limited on the ground,
in this clearing where the field is ringed

by a rampart of trees. Lock the target. I have
no target. Trust your hearing, he repeats.
And when I say hawk before its shadow
crosses over our heads, before sound or sight
can confirm it, I am labeled prey

instead of hunter. The joke is that only a bird
senses the presence of a stronger bird.
You are prey, he laughs. *You're a strange bird.*
When I turn quickly and fire my rifle over his head,
a distant dove suddenly forced to contend with gravity,

my shy hunter is as pale as an apparition. A rifle is
an extension of the man, I respond. Somewhere
in the distance, the hawk wheels and disappears
into a stand of trees. Despite everything, he is right,
my shy hunter. I know this. I know I am prey.

Money

Women want to save you or want you to savage them.
Men want to see what is under your towel.
The dollar bills they throw into your cage
are all you need to care about because
you aren't dancing in a cage to entertain them.

You dance in a cage to make money. I open
my towel to the right then whip it back toward midline
just as I open to the left: I show them nothing.
But I have them convinced I will show them something.
There is a difference between men and women—

you must look women in the eyes and, if possible,
look hurt; with men, you must avoid looking
at them altogether, you must focus on moving your hips,
which is close to what they are actually watching.
Suspended in a cage above the far end

of the dance floor, I was not attainable; I
made myself seem attainable. These are just the basics.
Wearing nothing but a towel, my greyish wings
extended to full wingspan, my chest shaved—
the clubbers believe I am wearing a costume.

It is amazing what people believe. The music
is cheaper than a Budweiser. The air is smoke and
the smell of smoke mixed with sweat, and your job
is to convince each of them you are dancing for no one else.
When my shift is over and I pull on some jeans,

tuck my wings and bandage them down, pull on two shirts,
I can almost pretend I never entered that cage in the first place.
Outside on Lansdowne Street, there are people standing
in one line or another waiting to get in to clubs.
Night after night, the same thing: the waiting never ends.

The Wolf

From the warm blues of the Caribbean,
twisting funnels of salt water vanish
as they quietly move north, vanish the way fish do
when they sense danger, when a predator is
nearby, these funnels in aggregate referred to as

a stream, the Gulf Stream, its purpose, I was told
as a child, to keep England temperate; and out
off the Cape nothing remotely blue in this
interminable sleeve of seawater. You want to
find something borrowed, something blue, a bit

of sky or sky reflected in the dim waves limping
ashore. Instead, you find these waters off shore
to be lost and grey and anything but inviting—
some say you find what you are meant to find.
The trees in the distance behind you

are an embarrassment of color:
yellows, yellows, ambers and rusts,
leaves trying to compensate
for what a novice might call
blustery weather, but not even salt air

can distract from all of this color
behind us. One leaf, an almost
iridescent green-going-gold looks as if
someone has held a match to its edges.
Imagine. But who has time to stop

and study a leaf? Who has time to
slow down when the ocean's slapdash
of waves is in front of you? Grey, the sand,
and grey the odd rocks on this sand
as if color were too expensive,

the trees behind us the only things
able to afford such a gaudy display.
Goodbye to those adequate streets
of Boston, streets that change
their names more than once

even in a short distance, a city designed
more for livestock and walking
than for the modern era, and goodbye, too,
to those two-lane roads that brought us here.
To travel is to rid oneself of oneself,

or so I remember the old Jesuit mumbling
in front of our lecture hall, half the students
asleep or dreaming of the night's decadence
ahead of them. Yes, something about losing
oneself, losing the habits of a life.

I don't know if I lost myself on the Cape,
but after those two-lane roads with their rickety
fences lining parts of them, after clapboard
and signs having more and more
of a nautical theme, the seafood restaurants...

I don't know. One thing after another
flickered by. And then, the small cottage,
grey, of course, looking barely habitable.
On the left, woods, and on the right
a path to the ocean, path cleared

by footfall of visitors and nothing more.
Feeling the need to flee those who would
likely say we were all friends, the four
of us having survived that drive and
the faulty directions, I take the path

to the beach. I suppose I was trying
to lose myself. Coming up the path,
a shirtless young man wearing a backpack
carrying yellow leaves as if they were a bouquet:
Quiet day, today, very quiet. Not too much going on

down by the dunes. What can one do but smile
in such circumstances, especially when
you have no idea what this hiker
is talking about. Of course, it is quiet. After
the yellows—the dimmer pale yellows and

more vibrant yellows—rusts
and occasional oranges, those being rare
somehow, so unlike the Public Gardens
where reds and oranges are anything
but scarce, the beach and

then ocean come into view. I want to
lose myself the way a cousin did one
afternoon in late spring. She went out
after lunch, swam in the sea and then
disappeared. We were six then,

and although the adults cried, it seemed
amazing that one could vanish
into thin air. Imagine. But the grey
beach, the grey water, the grey rocks,
the grey man fishing in the distance,

none of it seemed worthwhile.
Back up the path toward the cottage,
back through the trees holding their
bright fans out for birds, for all
of us, really, back past the cottage

and into the evergreens, not so much
a path as many small paths, those evergreens
having carpeted the ground in needles,
an abundance of needles, squirrels
bounding over this carpet busy with

the work of squirrels, which is confusing
but seemingly endless. Quiet day, quiet
occasionally cut by birdsong, rare though, as if
the birds had lost themselves inside
these woods. Suddenly, not birdsong

but footfall. And in a clearing up ahead,
a man has come out of the denser woods
and stands in a clearing. Is he
a lumberjack? If so, where is his axe?
From the look of him, he must be

a lumberjack, his shoulders broad,
his bared chest muscular. He stands there
and stares up the path, glares really,
his eyes somehow intent on surveying the path
and anything on it, including me.

Who knows why one senses danger? We both
stand there. The waiting seems to last forever.
We stand there and face each other down. If he
was trying to lose himself, I have ruined it,
having found him. He doesn't hurry. He

doesn't move. And when he lifts his head
and howls like a werewolf in a B movie, I want
to howl back, but I am not sure if that is how
one responds to such a greeting. And he
howls again, as if to challenge me.

Even at that distance, I could make out
sweat on his hairy chest and along his neck.
He is dangerous. And when there is
the sound of something else in the woods,
the sense of danger builds, and neither of us moves.

When a branch tumbles to the ground, I jump,
feel panic as the wings begin tearing through the muscles
between my shoulder blades, my wings erupting now
like a B movie, my wings ripping my shirt open
at the back, the force of it so painful I cry out.

The man quietly watches all of this and then runs back
into the dense wood. He doesn't turn back,
and he doesn't howl again. He vanished. Imagine.
That old Jesuit lied, as adults are apt to do. We lose
so many things in this life, but we never lose ourselves.

Revelation

Running through the forest, I felt eyes tracking me.
I tested it. I made turn after turn, ran faster, much faster
than any man or animal. Something continued tracking
me, continued to match my speed and cornering.
And when I stopped to turn, a man rushed at me,

struck me in the chest with the bare side of his forearm:
backward, backward, arch and then fall, the wind
forced from my chest, the impact strong enough to turn
my body into a ballistic that felled a small pine tree.
Struggling for breath, my heart so quick in my chest it hurt,

I rose and faced this man, a man much older than me.
When he rushed again, I struck him in his neck,
cycled and wheeled out of his path. This went on
forever, the fighting, each one hurling himself at the other,
gasping and huffing, fists thrown, fists made weapon,

the speed of it at times blurring our motions. When he
finally spoke, all he said was *Show yourself. Show me.*
And when I refused to respond, when I stood there
with eyes locked on him, he pulled his shirt over his
head, his face purpling with rage. And then, it happened,

his wings presenting themselves behind him, the feathers
quill-like and grey, feathers similar to the ones I have studied
in the mirror for so many years. *Show yourself.*
And surprised my own wings hadn't already erupted,
I removed my shirt and felt the tearing heat to which

I have long since grown accustomed. We faced
each other, two unabashed winged things. We lunged.
We struck. We wrestled. The fight went on for hours.
And when we declared a draw, the two of us cut and bruised,
each of us out of breath and crouching, I stared at him.

Even then, we dared not take our eyes off each other.
He could not be trusted. I could not be trusted. And when
I finally had enough breath to speak, when I asked him if he
were a god, he answered *Are you?* We rose. We
backed away from the other. I rephrased the question,

asked him what kind of thing I was. He backed further
and further away, his eyes never leaving mine. And when he
tucked his wings, pulled his shirt back on, he shouted *Human.*
You are just human. He turned and disappeared into the woods.
Only then did I truly understand the cruelty of the gods.

Human Wishes

In order to prove to a hunter you are not
prey, you have to kill him. It's that simple.
There are no *ifs ands* or *buts* about it.
My shy hunter was a model for me, a model
of a man. But I am not a man.

An accident, some kind of hybrid, I am a monster.
I thank the generous god who prompted wings
from inside my back, thank the god who
gave me the keenness of sight, my ability
to harness all of my senses, gave me speed.

I thank the drunk woman who ran a red light,
the result being deep sleep, thank her for
crippling me, for leaving three cracks in the bone
to be seen on an x-ray. I thank the many failures
that came of these events, because I am a grateful

thing. I am grateful. I wanted most of all to be a man,
an ordinary man. I suppose that is the most human
aspect of me, the want. Real men hunt. So, what choice
did I have but to apprentice myself to this hunter?
My shy hunter says *Tell me what you see in the field.*

And I do. I catalog hiding places. I list off
potential targets without batting an eye.
When I list him as one of the things I see,
his only response is to chuckle and remind me
he is a person and not a thing, not an animal.

There are no *ifs ands* or *buts* about it.
You already know what happens. You already know
how this story ends. How could you not? I removed
my shirt, the bandages, too. My wings unfurled.
And when I raised the rifle and told him to run, he ran.

The Halo

In the paintings left to us
by the Old Masters, the halo,
a smallish cloud of light, clung
to the head, carefully framed the faces
of mere mortals made divine.

Accident? My body launched
by a car's incalculable momentum?
It ended up outside the car. I had no idea then
what it was like to lose days, to wake
and find everything had changed.

Through glass, this body went
through the glass window, the seatbelt
snapping my neck. Not the hanged man,
not a man made divine but more human.
I remember those pins buried in my skull,

the cold metal frame surrounding my head,
metal reflecting a small fire, a glow. All
was changed. In that bed, I was a locust.
I was starving. And how could I not be?
I, I . . . I am still ravenous.

Acknowledgments

Grateful acknowledgment is made to the editors of the following publications, where these poems—sometimes in slightly different form—first appeared:

Academy of American Poets website, American Poetry Review, The Awl, Boston Review, Chronicle of Higher Education, Connotation Press: An Online Artifact, The Collagist, Descant, diode, Kenyon Review, Linebreak, The Paris-American, Plume, Southwest Review, Subtropics, Virginia Quarterly Review, and *Waccamaw.*

"The Hanged Man" was reprinted in *The Rag-Picker's Guide to Poetry*, eds. Eleanor Wilner and Maurice Manning. (University of Michigan Press, 2013).

"The Second Fallacy" was reprinted as a broadside by *Broadsided*, ed. Elizabeth Bradfield. (April 2014).

As always, I would like to thank my beloved, Jacob Bertrand. I would also like to thank my family and friends for the incredible support they have given me. I specifically want to thank Rick Barot, Christopher Castellani, Geri Doran, and Jennifer Grotz. To my medical practice partner, Lisa Boohar, I am beyond grateful for her understanding of the time I have taken to do this work, year in and year out.

Significant gratitude is owed to the John Simon Guggenheim Memorial Foundation for a fellowship that allowed me the time to bring this collection into being. I owe a debt of gratitude to The MacDowell Colony for a Kate and George Kendall Fellowship that provided me the perfect setting to complete the poems for this collection and to the Rockefeller Foundation for a Literary Arts Fellowship at the Villa Serbelloni/ Bellagio Center, where I assembled and revised this collection. And finally, I would like to thank my editor Martha Rhodes and everyone at Four Way Books for their continued belief in my work.

C. Dale Young practices medicine full-time and teaches in the Warren Wilson MFA Program for Writers. He is the author of *The Day Underneath the Day* (Northwestern, 2001), *The Second Person* (Four Way Books, 2007) a finalist for the Lambda Literary Award in Poetry, and *Torn* (Four Way Books 2011), named one of the best poetry collections of 2011 by National Public Radio. He is a previous recipient of the Grolier Prize, the Stanley W. Lindberg Award for Literary Editing, as well as fellowships from the Corporation of Yaddo, the MacDowell Colony, the National Endowment for the Arts, the John Simon Guggenheim Memorial Foundation, and the Rockefeller Foundation. His poems and short fiction have appeared in many anthologies and magazines, including *Asian-American Poetry: The Next Generation*, several installments of *The Best American Poetry*, *Legitimate Dangers: American Poets of the New Century*, *American Poetry Review*, *The Atlantic Monthly*, *Guernica*, *The Nation*, *The New Republic*, and *The Paris Review*. He lives in San Francisco with his spouse Jacob Bertrand.

Publication of this book was made possible by grants and donations. We are also grateful to those individuals who participated in our 2015 Build a Book Program. They are:

Jan Bender-Zanoni, Betsy Bonner, Deirdre Brill, Carla & Stephen Carlson, Liza Charlesworth, Catherine Degraw & Michael Connor, Greg Egan, Martha Webster & Robert Fuentes, Anthony Guetti, Hermann Hesse, Deming Holleran, Joy Jones, Katie Childs & Josh Kalscheur, Michelle King, David Lee, Howard Levy, Jillian Lewis, Juliana Lewis, Owen Lewis, Alice St. Claire Long & David Long, Catherine McArthur, Nathan McClain, Carolyn Murdoch, Tracey Orick, Kathleen Ossip, Eileen Pollack, Barbara Preminger, Vinode Ramgopal, Roni Schotter, Soraya Shalforoosh, Marjorie & Lew Tesser, David Tze, Abby Wender, and Leah Nanako Winkler